Help Your Child

King Kangaroo

ALLAN AHLBERG and ANDRÉ AMSTUTZ

GRANADA
London Toronto Sydney New York

Help Your Child To Read

Parents can help their children to start reading. It is not difficult, nor is it necessary to be a trained teacher. In many ways home is a better place to start than school. In school your child will share the teacher's time with 25 or 30 others. At home he can have your undivided attention.

The series HELP YOUR CHILD TO READ is a set of books for parents to share with their children. The books contain stories, rhymes and games. Also, on page 3 of each book, there are practical suggestions for parents: ways in which they can help their children to start reading.

First Words

Probably the most important words to a young child are: mummy, daddy, and his own name. To help your child to read these words, try this:

1. Write mummy on a postcard. Say, "This is the word 'mummy'." Attach a string to the card; wear it (briefly!).
2. Get dad to make a 'daddy' card.
3. When your child is familiar with (can 'read') mummy and daddy, make a card with his name on it.
4. Later, supply a verb, e.g. kisses/hugs/chases. Lay the cards in a row and act out the resulting sentences: daddy hugs Tom.

There's a lolly
in my pocket –
Oh, what shall I do?

Suck it and see
O King Kangaroo!

There are balloons
in my pocket –
paper hats too
and an odd kind of package.
Oh, what shall I do?

Put a hat on your head
that's what you should do,
and we'll play
pass the parcel
O King Kangaroo!

There's a jelly
in my pocket,
a sandwich or two,
knives, forks and spoons –
serviettes too –
even a teapot.
Oh, what shall I do?

Leave it to us
that's what you should do.

We'll soon lay the table
O King Kangaroo!

There's a dog
in my pocket,
it really is true!
Some rabbits and pigeons,
Oh, what shall I do?
There's a conjuror's hat
and a conjuror too!

Just laugh at his tricks
that's what you should do,
and guess how he does them
O King Kangaroo!

There's a cake
in my pocket –
a cake-stand too!
What <u>is</u> going on?
I haven't a clue.

There's icing and candles!
Oh, what shall I do?

Take a big breath
and blow –
that's what you should do –
and we'll sing
Happy Birthday
O King Kangaroo!

Happy birthday
birthday to you,
happy birthday,

to you, happy
happy birthday,
O King Kangaroo!

Teapot

Lolly

Balloon

Hat

Cake

Dog

Pigeon

Jelly

Published by Granada Publishing Limited in 1983
ISBN 0 246 11859 8 (cased)
0 583 30550 4 (limp)

Granada Publishing Limited
Frogmore, St Albans, Herts AL2 2NF
and
36 Golden Square, London W1R 4AH
515 Madison Avenue, New York, NY 10022, USA
117 York Street, Sydney, NSW 2000, Australia
60 International Blvd, Rexdale, Ontario, R9W 6J2, Canada
61 Beach Road, Auckland, New Zealand

Printed and bound in Spain by
Graficas Reunidas S.A., Madrid